NEW LOVE
Study Guide

Your Handbook for Beginning Your Life as One

Dr. Frank and Mary Alice Minirth
Dr. Brian and Dr. Deborah Newman
Dr. Robert and Susan Hemfelt
Compiled by Gary Wilde

A JANET THOMA BOOK

THOMAS NELSON PUBLISHERS
NASHVILLE

Other Books in This Series

Realistic Love Study Guide
Steadfast Love Study Guide
Renewing Love Study Guide
Transcendent Love Study Guide

The case examples presented in this book are fictional composites based on the authors' clinical experience with thousands of clients through the years. Any resemblance between these fictional characters and actual persons is coincidental. Two of the six authors, Mary Alice Minirth and Susan Hemfelt, are not psychotherapeutic clinicians and are not associated with the Minirth-Meier Clinic. The contributions of Mary Alice Minirth and Susan Hemfelt are derived from personal experience and their contribution makes no claim of professional expertise. Portions of this book that address clinical theory and clinical perspectives do not include contributions from Mary Alice Minirth and Susan Hemfelt.

Since many readers may read only one book in this series, we have repeated key concepts in more than one book. If you encounter this repetition, please be open to the possibility that these subjects are so vital, they bear such repetition.

Published in Nashville, Tennessee, by Thomas Nelson, Inc., and distributed in Canada by Lawson Falle, Ltd., Cambridge, Ontario.

Scripture quotations are from the NEW KING JAMES VERSION of the Bible. Copyright © 1979, 1980, 1982, Thomas Nelson, Inc., Publishers.

Library of Congress Cataloging-in-Publication Data

New love study guide / Frank and Mary Alice Minirth . . . [et al.] ; compiled by Gary Wilde.
    p.   cm.
    ISBN 0-8407-4562-1
    1. Marriage—Religious aspects—Christianity. I. Minirth, Frank B. II. Wilde, Gary.
BV835.N49 1993
248.8'44—dc20   92-26099
                                                     CIP

Printed in the United States of America

1 2 3 4 5 6—97 96 95 94 93

Contents

Introducing the
Passages Study Guides

You've made an excellent decision! You've decided to take some time out of your busy schedule in the next few weeks to focus on something that is very important to you, something that often gets taken for granted: your marriage. Your decision will launch you into an exploration of where you are in your "marital journey" and help you successfully navigate the next passages along your route to a more healthy, loving relationship with your spouse.

For Individual Study

As you work through the questions in this study guide, you will review and apply the principles taught in the Thomas Nelson book *Passages of Marriage,* by Frank and Mary Alice Minirth, Brian and Deborah Newman, and Robert and Susan Hemfelt. The Scripture readings and discussion questions will provide you with an excellent, non-threatening entry into marriage enrichment. (If possible, get your spouse involved with you in this study, too.)

The five passages of a marriage are: (1) New Love, referred to as Young Love in the *Passages* book, the first two years; (2) Realistic Love, the third through the tenth years; (3) Steadfast

Love, the eleventh through the twenty-fifth years; (4) Renewing Love, the twenty-sixth through the thirty-fifth years; (5) Transcendent Love, the thirty-sixth year and on. This guide talks about the five specific tasks of Young Love. Each chapter considers one of those tasks. By tasks we mean "attitude changes one must make and jobs one must complete in order to maintain an intimate marital relationship."

The introductory paragraphs in each study present the concept you will be considering. After jotting your personal reactions to this concept, you'll study and apply a portion of Scripture related to the topic. Finally, you'll spend some time in prayer, praising God for insights gained and asking Him for greater strength to carry out what you've learned. Here, then, is how the three main sections of the study guide move you through this process:

1. My Story: The questions in this section emphasize personal reflection. You'll recall the particular task of marriage you've considered: What insights, issues, or questions formed in my mind in response to the material? What past experiences do I remember that help me relate to the authors' examples? In what ways did my reading offer a new vision of my future role as a spouse?

2. God's Story: A natural progression in Christian growth is to first consider where I am, then consider God's call to me, then decide where I need to move in order to live closer to His revealed will daily. The coming together of My Story and God's Story creates some healthy inner tension. And you'll benefit from this challenging form of self-discovery as it spurs you to make positive changes in attitude and actions.

The first three or four questions in this section relate directly to the Bible passage. They ask you to explore the content of God's Word and to consider its personal meaning for you and your marriage. You will ask yourself questions like: What does this passage tell me about God's will for human relationships? How do these biblical principles relate to my relationship with my spouse? What do I find here that is intriguing, challenging, or convicting?

The next set of questions help you apply what you have learned from the Bible to one of the five tasks of Young Love.

Here you'll analyze your marital relationship, based on the tasks required of those in your particular marriage passage.

3. Prayer Moments: As you read and study, you will no doubt realize that you have successfully completed some of the tasks in your marriage passage. This is cause for great joy. However, you will also recognize areas of your marriage that need strengthening. This study guide invites you to take some time to bring both your joys and your ongoing concerns before the Lord in prayer. You may wish to use the suggested prayer-time format or offer prayer in your own customary manner.

If You Are Studying with a Group

You may be using this guide along with a group of other couples who are in the same stage of marital development as you are. Your group may be led by a facilitator, or the group may choose to rotate leadership responsibilities weekly. Each chapter of the guide covers a key element, or task, in your group's passage of marriage so everyone can be ready to join in group discussion. (See "Leading the Passages Studies," at the back of this guide, for detailed instructions on how to facilitate a group study of Passages.)

The key to enjoying a study series with others is to enter into discussion wholeheartedly. Be willing to share about yourself, your ideas, and your particular struggles at appropriate times. As you and others risk truthfully revealing who you are, you will find yourselves growing closer together in a deepening bond of fellowship. Listening and responding to others' experiences will give you a more objective view of your own problems. You'll see that you are not alone in any of your struggles to maintain a healthy marriage; others have been where you are. People in your group will offer valuable insights, and you, in the same way, can aid others by sharing from your learned wisdom.

Most groups will have a good sense of how to relate to each other during the series of studies. However, it's probably best to make these assumptions explicit by putting them in an

informal statement, or covenant, to which all can subscribe.
Such a covenant could include a few standard guidelines like:

- Regular attendance: I commit to being here for each
  meeting unless an emergency situation calls me away. If I
  know I will miss a meeting, I will inform the leader in
  advance, if possible.
- Promise of confidentiality: I will hold in strict confidence
  the items of personal sharing revealed in these meetings.
- Spirit of participation: I will seek to become fully involved in conversation and sharing, as I feel led and as I
  feel comfortable.
- Direct, loving communication: I will seek to maintain
  personal integrity by letting others know when I sense a
  problem in the way the group is relating to me.
- Willingness to be available: I will try to be available for
  others when they express a need for practical help or
  nurture. My phone number is _____.
- Other guidelines for your group: _____.
- Referral to professional assistance: If I recognize in myself or other group members the presence of serious individual or marital distress, I will encourage that person to
  seek competent professional mental health care.

Other Books in This Series

Each book in this series of study guides based on the passages of Marriage describes in detail one of the stages of marital development. The books explain both the joys and potential hazards of each stage while giving clear, practical advice
about how to navigate through those problem areas. Each of
the marital stages demands the completion of specific tasks
before a couple can move to the next stage. Where are you?
What is your next task as a couple?

"You Don't Marry a Dream . . . You Marry a Person"

Old movies make it look so easy: Man carries woman over threshold. Marital bliss begins. Love, romance, excitement—they're definitely headed for "happily ever after." But can two independent persons really mold themselves into one loving family unit? That is the challenge of the very first passage of marriage. It's a time of high idealism and romantic dreams. But it holds the potential for devastating disappointment.

Regardless of what the couple think about how well they know each other, they still face the problem of superficial intimacy. They just haven't had the time yet to get to know each other well. Yet, they must balance their desire to make an all-out commitment to the new marriage with their wish to keep old friends. They must break strong ties to the original families while nurturing a relationship with in-laws (who may be working overtime to keep the familial strings firmly attached!). All of this requires huge doses of patience along with myriad attitude adjustments beginning on the first day of that sparkling, brand-new marriage.

Before long, the walls of the new marital home resound with "Who's in control here?" The resulting conflict will be scary. If a couple succumb to their fears, they'll retreat to the various ways of avoiding conflict rather than learning to view it as a potential asset, another route into the depths of intimacy. They can, if they work at it, learn to compromise, agree to disagree, and even give in as a free, unforced gift of love.

Perhaps the most daunting challenge in the first two years is the task of transforming a dreamlike, dating-years romance into a deeply caring, mature love, including a satisfying sexual union. By pursuing greater intimacy on every level, a couple begin building a solid marital foundation, one that can weather the storms of conflict that are sure to come.

Every couple in the first two years, then, must make responsible choices based on a primary commitment to stick with the marriage. The temptation may be to "run for the hills." One or both of the partners may feel they've trapped themselves in a poor choice. Perhaps both partners struggle with inherited unfinished business from the incomplete marriage passages of their parents. Can they sit down and talk these things through?

Couples find their own unique ways to either withdraw from these challenges or to move forward in marital development. The ones who make it through the first passage of marriage have always learned to adjust, to compromise, to risk the vulnerability required for a deepening intimacy. They have not resisted change or pretended things were okay when they really weren't. As one veteran of years of marriage said to his newlywed son-in-law: "You're gonna grow, regardless. So when you see yourself growing apart, sit down and figure out how to grow together."

Chapter 1

What Are the Passages of Marriage?

I t's a solid hit into deep right field!" the announcer screams exuberantly. "The ball is still airborne as the player rounds first. The ball drops into tall grass. . . . The player passes third, homeward bound."

Wait! He failed to touch second! As his team groans in unison, he runs back to stomp second base. What would have been a home run ends up only a double, all because the runner failed to clear second base satisfactorily. Marriage is like that. We call the bases "passages."

First things first, right? You touch second before you race for third; you buckle up before you pull out of the driveway; you check your parachute before jumping out of the plane.

Passages of Marriage tells us that it's first things first in the married life, too. There are at least five distinct stages of development that every marriage must eventually navigate if it is to remain healthy and happy throughout it's life. Each of these passages requires a couple to accomplish specific tasks before they can enter the next stage, regardless of the couple's age or the length of their marriage.

Of course, you need to know and understand what the tasks are before you can work on completing them. You need to ask yourself: How do these tasks relate to me and my unique marital journey?

My Story

1. By choosing this study guide, you have determined that you are in the marital passage of New Love. What is your initial guess about the most pressing marital task(s) you need to accomplish at this point? Check one or more of these tasks (which you will be studying in the weeks ahead):

____ Task One: Mold into One Family
____ Task Two: Stop Jockeying for Control
____ Task Three: Build a Sexual Union
____ Task Four: Make Responsible Choices
____ Task Five: Deal with Your Parents' Passages

2. "Any emotional or psychological difficulty in one marital partner will invariably influence, and be influenced by, the other partner. Always." How would you assess your own psychological health? (For instance, "I've been struggling with an incident of sexual abuse in my childhood that has caused me great anxiety.")

3. How would you assess your spouse's psychological health? (For instance, "My spouse is working through grief because of a parent's recent death.")

4. Name some marital problems or issues that have arisen because of anxiety, depression, or forms of codependency on

the part of either partner. (For instance, "My spouse still refuses to admit to alcohol addiction.")

God's Story
2 Peter 1:2–8

Grace and peace be multiplied to you in the knowledge of God and of Jesus our Lord, as His divine power has given to us all things that pertain to life and godliness, through the knowledge of Him who called us by glory and virtue, by which have been given to us exceedingly great and precious promises, that through these you may be partakers of the divine nature, having escaped the corruption that is in the world through lust. But also for this very reason, giving all diligence, add to your faith virtue, to virtue knowledge, to knowledge self-control, to self-control perseverance, to perseverance godliness, to godliness brotherly kindness, and to brotherly kindness love. For if these things are yours and abound, you will be neither barren nor unfruitful in the knowledge of our Lord Jesus Christ.

1. In this Scripture passage, Peter describes the Christian life as a developmental process. In the same way that our marriages must continue to develop, we grow spiritually as we add various personal traits to our lives: faith, virtue, knowledge, self-control, perseverance, godliness, kindness, love. Pick one of these traits and imagine it being much more evident in your marital relationship. Tell how, specifically, this trait could help you overcome a problem in your marriage.

2. If you were to choose the key Christian trait(s) characterizing your marriage right now, which would you pick?

Which of the traits in the list would you, personally, like to display to a greater degree?

3. Through God's power we have been given "all things that pertain to life and godliness." Name at least two areas of your marriage that could benefit from a new reliance on God's power or help. Describe how you would like to see God work in those areas.

4. Every marriage changes with time. Some changes are for the better and some are not. What changes have you seen in your marriage in the past year that improved your relationship to your spouse? (Name some changes, too, that tended to stress or weaken your relationship.)

5. "Our very nature throws into our marriage certain clinkers that we do not recognize and cannot anticipate." These clinkers (or "time-release capsules" from our past) can be turned from bad to good if we can find and manage the sources of trouble. What may be some of the time-release

capsules that could "go off" in your marriage, related to the potential problem areas the authors suggest?

Chronic financial stress:

In-law problems and involvement:

Family imbalance and stress:

Emotional or psychological dysfunctions:

Other area(s):

6. The tasks that accompany a particular marital passage must be completed before the tasks of the next passage can commence. By tasks we mean "attitude changes one must make and jobs one must complete in order to maintain an intimate marital relationship." In what ways have you

found that maintaining a healthy marriage requires some hard work?

7. When a marriage gets stuck in a passage, each partner, as an individual, ceases to grow, too. Name some ways you have sought to advance your personal growth during the last year (emotional, spiritual, or intellectual).

How has your personal growth (or lack of it) affected the growth of your marriage relationship?

8. Imagine a "typical" couple, Rick and Jenny, who are in your passage of marriage. For some time they have been confronting three common, but serious, marital challenges: fighting about money, making factional alliances with parents and in-laws, and struggling with sexual dysfunction. If you were asked to recommend an initial step in solving this couple's problems, what would your advice be?

Prayer Moments

LORD, thank You for Your provision of the strength and help I need to fulfill my role in marriage. The most challenging task for me at this stage of my marriage is:

I ask Your help to:

Amen.

Chapter 2

Task One: Mold into One Family

In shifting to their new family and in putting original family patterns behind, the couple in the first flush of young love must completely reshape all their other relationships. Finding the new balance point is inevitably rocky. You've never seen such wild flailing and tilting!

Someone once described the transition to married life like this: "The difference between courtship and marriage is the difference between the pictures in the seed catalog and what comes up." The variation between what is promoted and what is experienced can be quite startling. Does it really have to be that way?

Considering the obstacles we face upon entering a brand-new marriage, we may ask why anyone would ever have promoted it as easy:

- putting the original family patterns behind us;
- developing new family patterns from the melding of two unique personalities;
- coming to terms with divergent attitudes about money, communication, religion, household responsibilities, sexual fulfillment.

All of this while learning to say goodbye to childhood pain. In this study you'll look at the Bible's account of the very first marriage in history. Surely the original couple faced some of the same challenges and tasks of anyone in this Young Love passage of marriage. In some ways, perhaps, they had it easier. They started with a perfect relationship to the Creator. However, they were mere human beings like us. To "become one flesh," they, too, needed to make some major adjustments.

My Story

1. The first task of young love is to mold into one family. For you, what is the most challenging aspect of this task? (For instance, "I struggle with my desire always to go back to my mother for advice about my marriage.")

2. "Regardless of what the couple think, their intimacy in the beginning is superficial." What evidence of superficial intimacy do you find in your marriage? (For instance, "I can't seem to talk with my spouse about sex." "My spouse gets uncomfortable or irritated when I share anything other than 'positive' or 'happy' feelings.")

3. Every marriage is like a three-legged stool: husband; wife; and the third leg, which changes and regularly gets kicked out. There can be positive third-leg supports such as each individual's relationship with God. There can also be distracting third-leg activities such as a spouse's overinvolvement in a career or hobby. As you look ahead, what positive "third leg" issues run the risk of being kicked out from under

you and what potentially distracting third-leg issues threaten your intimacy? (For instance, "I can envision problems ahead when I start taking night school classes after work.")

God's Story
Genesis 2:18–25

And the LORD God said, "It is not good that man should be alone; I will make him a helper comparable to him." Out of the ground the LORD God formed every beast of the field and every bird of the air, and brought them to Adam to see what he would call them. And whatever Adam called each living creature, that was its name. So Adam gave names to all cattle, to the birds of the air, and to every beast of the field. But for Adam there was not found a helper comparable to him. And the LORD God caused a deep sleep to fall on Adam, and he slept; and He took one of his ribs, and closed up the flesh in its place. Then the rib which the LORD God had taken from man He made into a woman, and He brought her to the man. And Adam said:

> "This is now bone of my bones
> And flesh of my flesh;
> She shall be called Woman,
> Because she was taken out of Man."

Therefore a man shall leave his father and mother and be joined to his wife, and they shall become one flesh. And they were both naked, the man and his wife, and were not ashamed.

---

1. God said that "it is not good that [human beings] should be alone." Name some ways you experienced loneli-

ness before marriage. How has your marriage met some of your needs for intimacy?

2. How do you think Adam felt upon first seeing Eve?

How did you feel when you first met your future spouse?

What surprises or changes in first impressions came later? Describe any disappointment you felt.

3. How are you and your spouse leaving your father and mother (in the sense that is commanded in v. 24)?

In what ways would you say you are still tied to your parents in unhealthy ways?

4. To "become one flesh" reveals God's plan for marital intimacy. Though you and your spouse have become one flesh physically, in what specific areas would you now like to deepen your emotional intimacy?

5. "The happy newlyweds are certain that in each other their lives are complete." In what ways have you come to learn that you and your spouse are not complete in yourselves?

6. "Often a couple inadvertently strains their fragile intimacy by loading it with burdens it cannot carry." Make a list of some of these burdens you have noticed in your own marriage, things that threaten the deepening of intimacy with your spouse.

7. "Love hunger" is a key concept in recovery counseling. Most of us, if we are honest, will admit to significant affection and nurture gaps in our childhood experience with parents. Every child longs to be held, affirmed, comforted—but not every child got those things, or enough of them. Julia expected Jerry to fill much of the love hunger she brought to the marriage from her childhood.

Be Jerry. How do you respond to Julia?

Be Julia. What steps can you take to begin dealing with your love hunger?

8. The doctors of the Minirth-Meier Clinic have found that the more dysfunctional and dissatisfactory a child's family has been, the harder it is for the child to leave it. List some ways your own family life seemed dissatisfactory to you. How have these things made it harder for you to leave your family of origin?

Prayer Moments

LORD, the thing that is most painful in putting my original family patterns behind me is:

I ask Your help to do a better job at:

Amen.

Chapter 3

Task Two: Stop Jockeying for Control

I n a famous short story, a man must choose between two doors. If he opens one, a willing and lovely lady awaits him. Behind the other door waits a hungry tiger. The story is an allegory of life, and it also typifies conflict. Behind one door is intimacy. Behind the other, separation. But there's an infinite difference here. The man cannot know in advance which door hides what. You can.

Conflict can go either way. Handled unwisely, it causes pain and separation. Used with skill, as an occasion for greater openness, it leads us onto the heavenly plains of emotional intimacy. It's a lady-and-the-tiger situation.

The danger is that we will avoid conflict completely because we know its great potential for hurt. The marriage that avoids hurt at all costs, however, becomes a sad caricature of a relationship. Two people who never fight never really get to know each other, never really live together. Is avoiding the pain of conflict really worth the price of alienation?

Young Lovers can learn to go through their conflicts to peaceful resolution. Every time conflict hits, they can unleash their skills, consider their options, make their choices—from compromising, to sharing a love gift. Happiness and contentment really are just behind that next door. Go ahead. Open!

My Story

1. Recall the last conflict you experienced with your spouse. Slowly review the situation, in detail, in your mind. How did you feel during your argument? (For instance, "I felt lonely, hopeless, ashamed.")

2. Can you remember the last time you felt that way growing up in your family of origin? (For instance, "I always felt lonely when my parents went on long business trips and left me at home." "My father always squelched my arguments with: 'That's enough out of you.' ")

3. If the two situations above are similar, describe some of their similarities. (For instance, "I feel as if I've been abandoned. Those feelings from childhood might be making me feel worse now.")

God's Story
John 13:3–17

Jesus, knowing that the Father had given all things into His hands, and that He had come from God and was going to God, rose from supper and laid aside His garments, took a towel and girded Himself. After that, He poured water into a basin and began to wash the disciples' feet, and to wipe them with the towel with which He was girded. Then He came to Simon Peter. And Peter said to Him, "Lord, are You washing my feet?" Jesus answered and said to him, "What I am doing you do not understand now, but you will know after this." Peter said to Him, "You shall never wash my feet!" Jesus answered him, "If I do not wash you, you have no part with Me." Simon Peter said to Him, "Lord, not my feet only, but also my hands and my head!" Jesus said to him, "He who is bathed needs only to wash his feet, but is completely clean; and you are clean, but not all of you." For He knew who would betray Him; therefore He said, "You are not all clean." So when He had washed their feet, taken His garments, and sat down again, He said to them, "Do you know what I have done to you? You call me Teacher and Lord, and you say well, for so I am. If I then, your Lord and Teacher, have washed your feet, you also ought to wash one another's feet. For I have given you an example, that you should do as I have done to you. Most assuredly, I say to you, a servant is not greater than his master; nor is he who is sent greater than he who sent him. If you know these things, happy are you if you do them."

---

1. This passage is a classic biblical illustration of true servanthood. What role could this type of servanthood play in your marriage relationship? Jot some specific examples.

2. In what way(s) was Peter "jockeying for control" in his conversation with Jesus?

How does the control issue usually surface between you and your spouse?

3. In our society, leadership can be described symbolically as a pyramid, with the power increasing the farther one goes up the ladder. What symbol would best express the Christian idea of leadership as demonstrated by Jesus?

What symbol would describe the form of leadership evident in your marriage, especially when you and your spouse make decisions?

4. "Not just expectations transfer from courtship into marriage. So does every unresolved issue." Name a conflict from courtship that you thought would disappear but seems to have blossomed now that you're married.

What has been the greatest barrier to resolving this conflict?

5. The authors point out that the greater our openness with our spouses, the greater the potential for either conflict or intimacy. Describe the last time you felt significant emotional intimacy as a result of openness with your spouse. What factors led to that experience?

How could this experience of intimacy be duplicated in the future by something you choose to do?

6. Part of the idealism of the Young Love stage of marriage is a feeling that "We shouldn't be fighting." If you have felt this way, how has your perspective changed as a result of working through this chapter on conflict?

7. "Dogs don't fight in support of ideas. They fight each other." What does this statement mean to you?

How does this principle apply to the pattern of conflicts in your marital relationship?

8. Recall once again the conflict situation you have experienced in the past (see question 1 under "My Story"). What could have been done to prevent its escalation? Use your new knowledge of conflict resolution options to answer this question.

Prayer Moments

LORD, fighting and arguing is no fun. The conflict situation that hurts me the most right now is:

I do thank You, though, for this one insight from You that can help me deal with future conflicts:

Amen.

Chapter 4

Task Three: Build a Sexual Union

L etting nature take its course would be sufficient were sex primarily biological. It is not. Unlike other biological needs—food, shelter, water—the sex drive is profoundly influenced by factors outside biology. The most active sex organ, and the least appreciated, is the brain. It does its thing largely beyond the conscious level.

In the movies and on TV the "one-night stand" has become a common—if not obligatory—standard for beginning a male-female relationship. But married people quickly come to realize that it takes more than one night to build sexual satisfaction into a truly intimate relationship. The wedding itself only sets the stage. Then, over the years, if a couple continue to grow in romance, they can expect the sexual side of their lives to mirror their overall happiness.

If the brain really is the most active sex organ, then every married couple can benefit from knowing how thoughts, feelings, and past experiences all play a role in the marriage bed. The brain can indeed promote meaningful sex. But it can also smother the flames of desire before the coals even begin to glow.

My Story

1. Men and women have different primary fears about the sexual aspect of marriage. Often the man fears that his sexual "performance" might fall short. The woman may fear that she will be unwanted sexually. Have you felt these fears in yourself? How? (For instance, "I have secretly felt my spouse was dissatisfied with my performance." "I've wondered why my spouse does not want sex more often.")

2. What actions or attitudes about sex from your family of origin might be influencing your married life? (For instance, "My mother taught me that sex was 'dirty' or 'not for nice girls.'")

3. Have you ever considered developing a Sexual Relationship Covenant with your spouse? What two or three points would you include in such a covenant as being essential for you? (For instance, "The covenant would have to affirm my right to say yes or no to a suggested sexual activity.")

God's Story
1 Corinthians 7:3–9

Let the husband render to his wife the affection due her, and likewise also the wife to her husband. The wife does not have authority over her own body, but the husband does. And likewise the husband does not have authority over his own body, but the wife does. Do not deprive one another except with consent for a time, that you may give yourselves to fasting and prayer; and come together again so that Satan does not tempt you because of your lack of self-control. But I say this as a concession, not as a commandment. For I wish that all men were even as I myself. But each one has his own gift from God, one in this manner and another in that. But I say to the unmarried and to the widows: It is good for them if they remain even as I am; but if they cannot exercise self-control, let them marry. For it is better to marry than to burn with passion.

___

1. Paul says we are to render due affection to our spouses. Do you feel you are getting the affection "due to you" from your spouse? Why or why not?

How well does your spouse know your feelings about this?

2. In what ways have you found it to be true that you really do not have "authority" over your own body in the marriage relationship?

3. This passage of Scripture tells us that we should "not deprive one another." Name some of the reasons why couples may end up depriving each other of sexual intimacy in their relationship.

If you have struggled with any of these problems, what key insight(s) did you get from your reading that could help you solve them?

4. "A man is turned on by what he sees, a woman by what she hears." How could you improve your basic approach to your spouse in order to enhance his or her enjoyment of sex?

What would you like to have your spouse pay more attention to, or improve, in this area?

5. For Sally, sex became a weapon of last resort. She unconsciously shut down her sexual responsiveness as a means of

expressing her resentment toward Steve for his apparent cold-
ness. If you sense that there might be deeper, unconscious
issues behind a sexual difficulty in your marriage, what might
those issues be?

Describe a scene in which you raise this issue as a topic of
conversation with your spouse. How would you begin the
conversation?

6. The Minirth-Meier doctors have found that a man or
woman abused in childhood always will suffer some degree of
sexual dysfunction in adulthood. If you are aware of any
forms of sexual abuse in your childhood, what is your attitude
to the idea of getting professional help to deal with this pain
from the past?

7. In meaningful sex, intimacy, as well as pleasure, is the
goal. This has been called "soul orgasm" or "emotional orgasm." What do you think is meant by these terms?

8. "Sex is love-making; romance is love-nurturing." When
was the last time you experienced love-nurturing romance
with your spouse?

How could you contribute to more such experiences in the future? Be practical and specific in your response.

Prayer Moments

LORD, thank You for creating sex. May I respond to my role in building a sexual union by:

I need more courage to talk openly with my spouse about my needs in this area, particularly about:

Amen.

Chapter 5

Task Four: Make Responsible Choices

There are few—if any—moral, social, or even ethical stigmas attached to divorce. We've lost the powerful peer pressures that used to keep people married." Bolt or stay? These are the two major choices, and there is no undoing the damage if you take the wrong fork.

Abandon ship! Abandon ship! (Or stay on board?) In this case you definitely want to make a responsible choice. Standing at the rail and looking down into that cold, lonely water, you'd like to know all about your chances for survival.

Setting aside for a moment the biblical proscriptions against abandoning your partner, the simple odds are that you'll be better off working to preserve your marriage than giving up on it. You do love each other, right? And you have made a huge commitment. You just need to know how to make that love and commitment work for you a little better.

Many people once tempted to split up will tell you, years later, that their determination to hold things together paid off in eventual marital peace and contentment. Of course, that's hard to accept when you're trying to swallow the bitter pill of disillusionment: "He's changed so much since the wedding"; "She seems so distant now that she's hooked me."

Yet those in Young Love have powerful resources to draw

upon as they face the urge to abandon ship. They can learn to confront their fears, adjust, compromise, keep the romance afloat.

My Story

Newlyweds experience a number of fears during the first few years of marriage. Name the fear behind each person's statement below, and then tell how you, personally, have experienced that fear.

1. "What's the big deal about intimacy? I want my space. . . . Too much intimacy messes up a relationship." (This statement shows the fear of vulnerability. "I've been afraid to talk with my spouse about my lack of self-confidence at work.")

2. "I'm stuck. I just bought into one marital partner for a lifetime. I just blew any chance to do better." (This statement shows a fear of entrapment. "I once told my spouse that I wished he could be more like my father.")

3. "That's it. No more. I'm going home to Mother." (This statement shows the fear of leaving home. "I usually call my mother before making even small decisions.")

God's Story
1 Corinthians 7:10–15

Now to the married I command, yet not I but the Lord: A wife is not to depart from her husband. But even if she does depart, let her remain unmarried or be reconciled to her husband. And a husband is not to divorce his wife. But to the rest I, not the Lord, say: If any brother has a wife who does not believe, and she is willing to live with him, let him not divorce her. And a woman who has a husband who does not believe, if he is willing to live with her, let her not divorce him. For the unbelieving husband is sanctified by the wife, and the unbelieving wife is sanctified by the husband; otherwise your children would be unclean, but now they are holy. But if the unbeliever departs, let him depart; a brother or a sister is not under bondage in such cases. But God has called us to peace.

---

1. This Bible passage commands married believers to remain married. Have you ever felt the urge to run from your marriage rather than stick it out? How have you handled your feelings?

2. Verse 11 deals with the possibility that a marriage partner might leave in order to marry someone else. If a separation does occur, what are the only two options left, according to Paul?

3. A man wanted a divorce in order to pursue a new love. As he began describing the situation, he told all about his

wife's failures and shortcomings while describing, in glowing terms, the wonderful qualities he saw in his new "find."

This man is on the brink of a major decision. Give some reasons why his plan may be a bad choice for him.

4. Making choices can be compared to a squirrel climbing a tree. The squirrel climbs up the trunk to the first major limb and is faced with a choice: Go out on this limb, or climb up toward the others. "Should the squirrel move out onto that bottom limb, a large part of the tree is out of reach, for it can't get to the rest of the tree from here." Good choices lead to fuller branches and happier times.

What is the most significant personal insight you gain from this "Choice Tree" analogy?

5. Poor choices lead us to dead-end branches, where we get stuck. Name some of the "branches" and "deadwood" you have been tempted to climb out on as you've moved up your own marital decision tree.

6. "The urge to run has never been easier to indulge than in the twentieth century." Do you agree? What would make it easy for you to run?

What things would make it hard for you to run?

7. Gretchen and Tim chose to pretend that their financial situation had not changed after leaving their affluent original families. They soon found themselves mired in debt, yet seemingly unable to control their spending. Are there any areas in which you and/or your spouse seem to be pretending?

If so, what responsible choices are now required?

8. Newlyweds find themselves at a fork in the road when "the new starts to wear off." What kinds of newness have worn off for you in the past year?

How have you seen the "real" spouse come through more clearly since your wedding?

9. How well would you say you've adjusted to the surprises as the "real" spouse has emerged? Give an example of something you've done, or plan to do, in this area of adjustment.

Prayer Moments

LORD, You have given me the strength to persevere in my marriage, even through difficult times. I especially thank You for the ability to:

Help me make the right choices as I face:

Amen.

Chapter 6

Task Five: Deal with Your Parents' Passages

P lay back the memories of your parents' disagreements. Then think about their actions. Any signs of war? It's your war as well as your parents' unless you give it back to them.

Our parents were our providers. If they were mostly responsible and unselfish, they gave us the things we needed to grow up: food, clothes, shelter, adequate amounts of affection. But parents hand down other things, too—attitudinal "gifts" we'd rather not carry with us into our adult lives. If only we could identify those things for the unwanted baggage they are! That's what this chapter is about: discovering and discarding the little packages of unfinished business we got from our parents.

We are called by Scripture to obey and honor our parents. We can do that, and we may very well want to do it. (The promise that goes with the command is a good incentive.) But we know that it would be wrong to continue our parents' marital neuroses in our own marriages. They may have stopped short in one of the marital passages and never moved on from there. We've got to pick up the ball and carry it further.

My Story

1. Think about the fights between your parents. Describe one that stands out most strongly, and tell how you felt during that fight.

What was the "known conflict" in this fight? (For instance, "They fought about how much time my father spent away from home on business.")

What do you suspect were the hidden conflicts or underlying fears just beneath the surface of most of your parents' fights? (For instance, "My mother was the youngest in a family of nine. I think she often felt ignored by her parents.")

2. "All incomplete passages become unfinished business for the next generation." What unfinished business are you aware of picking up from your parents? (For instance, "My parents never really said good-bye to their families of origin. I also have trouble breaking away.")

If you have children, what kinds of unfinished business might they inherit from you? (For instance, "They are probably picking up on my over-dependence on my parents' financial help.")

3. To what degree would you say you are now influenced by your parents' disappointments and disillusionments? Give an example to support your assessment. (For instance, "My father always wanted to earn more money than he did. He encourages me to go after the 'big deals' in my sales job.")

God's Story
Ephesians 6:1–4

Children, obey your parents in the Lord, for this is right. "Honor your father and mother," which is the first commandment with promise: "that it may be well with you and you may live long on the earth." And you, fathers, do not provoke your children to wrath, but bring them up in the training and admonition of the Lord.

1. What are some ways of honoring your parents without taking on their incomplete passages or unfinished business? Give a personal example.

2. How have your parents "provoked you to wrath" in the sense of leaving you with their unfinished business? Be specific.

3. What "unresolved negative gender stereotypes" have you picked up from your mother and father?

How have these stereotypes contributed to a continued battle of the sexes in your own marriage?

4. Can you see any evidence that, in choosing your mate, you made a "safe pick" in order to avoid replaying a weakness in your parents' marriage? Explain.

5. "You don't marry a dream or a way of life; you marry a person." Describe your dream-view of marriage before the wedding.

In what ways has your original vision been transformed (for "better" or "worse")?

6. In committing to growth, a couple should commit themselves to making no big decisions without thorough discussion. What was the last big decision made in your marriage?

Describe the process by which this decision was made.

How well did you work together with your spouse on this decision?

7. "Mom and Dad were surrogates for God. In a sense, they were God. Now they must be lifted from that pedestal." How dependent on your parents is your present God-image?

To what extent would you say your religious faith is either your own or depends on the influences of your family of origin? Explain.

What could you do to begin making your faith more your own?

8. The last time my spouse and I talked about our spiritual lives and/or prayed together was:

What one step could you take soon to develop your commitment to spiritual growth as a couple?

Prayer Moments

LORD, thank You for my parents. The hardest thing for me to accept about my relationship with them is:

I ask Your help to obey and honor my parents by:

Amen.

Leading the Passages Studies

Do you enjoy getting to know people through significant conversation? Do you want to strengthen your marriage through study and discussion with your spouse and with other couples? Would you like to share with others the things you've learned from experience and the Scriptures? Things that can help them, too? Leading a group through Passages of Marriage is a wonderful opportunity for you to do all of these things as you help others learn and grow.

Getting Started

You can use this study guide in a variety of settings and time frames. For instance, your group could meet weekly, bi-weekly, or monthly; it could meet in a home or during a Sunday school or mid-week hour at church. An informal home setting with minimal time constraint is probably best, however, since it will encourage a greater depth of sharing.

Consider having a low-key introductory meeting before launching into the sessions in this study guide. At this meeting you would distribute the study guides and give participants a chance to meet and get acquainted with each other. You could then offer a brief explanation of Passages of Marriage and talk about how you plan to proceed with the series. Get group members' comments and suggestions about how to schedule and structure your times together. Participants could then be asked to share some of their expectations for the sessions.

You may also wish to ask couples to "tell their stories" in this initial session. Give couples as much time as they want, even if you have to schedule some of the stories on different nights. Couples should share significant details about their early lives as individuals, their families of origin, how they met, and what they see as the "cutting-edge issue" in their marriages right now. Be sure each partner has a chance to talk. Ask specific questions of one of the partners, if necessary.

Ideally, you will have two to six couples in your group. Everyone should have a copy of both the Passages book and this study guide. Participants may read the appropriate pages from Passages during the week, or they may do the reading and fill in their guides together during the study time. It's up to you and your group to decide what will work best in light of peoples' home and work schedules. (Note: You may wish to invite some single participants, too—those who are contemplating marriage, or those who wish to review the history of a failed marriage in hopes of gaining skills for the future.)

Begin each session by reading the introductory paragraphs aloud to refresh group members' memories about the topic under study. If you have time, ask for personal reactions to the introduction. Then ask a volunteer to read the Bible passage aloud. (If you get no volunteers, read the passage yourself. Don't call on people; you'll risk embarrassing someone who is uncomfortable reading in public.) Proceed through each of the three main sections of the guide, drawing on the supplemental material found in the Leader's Notes for each study.

Use the discussion method of leading the group through the "My Story" and "God's Story" sections. Remember that adults thrive on discussion for a number of reasons: (1) it calls upon them to use and develop their analytical skills; (2) it lets them contribute from the storehouse of wisdom they've gained through years of experience; (3) it allows them to clarify and process what they've learned; and (4) it offers the opportunity to develop interpersonal skills that can enhance their marital communication.

The "Prayer Moments" section offers individuals the opportunity to jot their concerns and bring their desires before the Lord, privately. Use your knowledge of your group's unique personality to decide how, or whether, to use this section for group sharing and discussion. Some volunteers may wish to share what they have written; some groups may feel comfortable doing this every week. Other groups will simply structure a more general group prayer time that is comfortable for them.

Preparing for Group Leadership

As you prepare to lead, consider these five pieces of general advice that can promote any leader's success with a group:

- Study through all six of the sessions yourself, in advance, to get a good grasp of the Bible passages and a feel for the questions you'll want to emphasize in discussion. As you study, jot down points of particular interest or any ideas you have about how to deal with certain issues in a group setting. Formulate your own responses to the questions and recall events or stories from your experience that you could share with the group at appropriate points.
- Plan on including key ingredients for building a solid group life in your sessions. Structure some time for sharing and prayer. Perhaps offer light refreshments around which people can get to know each other socially before or after the study time.
- Decide how you will handle absenteeism. As leader, one of your responsibilities will be to follow up on those who miss sessions, letting them know they are missed. Find out if they foresee any problems getting to the next meeting. Ask if you can help them solve any problems with transportation, child care, and so on.

- Help your group members develop feelings of "closeness" as your study series unfolds. As the group members loosen up over the weeks, they'll begin feeling freer to share their real lives and struggles in meaningful ways. Be sure you include many of the sharing and application-type questions in every study. Don't limit your group to simply discussing "what the author said" without asking them to tell how they feel about it.
- Avoid group burnout. A group can get burned out when it never varies in intensity and seems to require a lifetime commitment. To counteract this potential problem, request short-term commitments for studies of deep intensity (like this six-session plan) and longer-term commitment for studies that involve less intensity. Be prepared to take chunks of "time off" between study series to give people a chance to assimilate what they've learned.

Using a Facilitator Approach

Act as a growth facilitator rather than as a "teacher" in leading these studies. A facilitating group leader provides a structure for igniting discussion and building friendships, stimulates participation through wise use of discussion questions, encourages and affirms others' attempts to learn and discuss, and models personal transparency by sharing about personal struggles as well as strengths. So, as a facilitator, you will find yourself summarizing group discussions and feelings, describing reactions of the group to ideas or issues, and helping the group go through conflict in productive ways. You can do all this if you simply have a desire to serve, a willingness to learn, and a commitment to spending significant time in preparation.

Note that the facilitator approach means a group leader is *not:*

- a person who always has the answer;
- a person who does most of the talking in the group;

- a person who takes total responsibility for everyone enjoying themselves;
- a person who perfectly displays, in his or her marriage, the principles being studied;
- a person who competes with others to produce the best ideas or to ask the most brilliant questions;
- a person who attempts to be a marriage therapist to other couples.

Working with Couples in a Group

You are not expected to be a marriage counselor during these sessions! However, knowing some basic principles of interpersonal relating can help you work with your couples:

- Let couples be themselves. There are many ways to live out a happy marriage, and each marital "contract" has its uniqueness. Accept people where they are and simply offer these studies as a means of exploring possible relational improvements in ways the couples themselves may decide upon.
- Learn to accept emotions expressed in the group. This particular study is quite different from the typical Bible study. Because couples will discuss aspects of their marriages, emotions will no doubt come into play. Let everyone know from the outset that emotions are normal and natural, though sometimes uncomfortable. If someone cries, offer a tissue, but do not ask the person to stop. Accept the tears, let them do their cleansing work, spend some time in silence, and move on in the discussion. Group members may offer appropriate comfort to the crying individual.
- Respond to possible conflict situations with helpful techniques. If individuals feel anger, it is entirely appropriate for them to "own" that anger and to state the reasons for it. However, ask group members to: (1) Use "I" statements when airing a complaint to a spouse ("I feel angry when this happens" rather than, "You make me

angry when . . .") An "I" statement shares about one's inner responses rather than being an attack on someone else. (2) Use the "and" method when offering a criticism. Often couples will say: "You do a great job at . . . but you don't. . . ." The second half of the statement tends to wipe out the first half. It's better if the *but* can be replaced with *and*. Then both statements can stand together with equal power. (3) Share how they feel. Help couples discuss crucial issues on more than just the intellectual level. They do need to understand certain things. But truth must have impact on the whole person if it is to lead to personal growth.

- Help group members apply important principles by occasionally asking, in a general way, "How could someone put this idea into practice?" You are taking some pressure off by making the application general and helping participants to envision it's outworking.

- Learn to use a "debriefing process" at points in your discussion. When couples share about a specific event or experience, help them go into more detail for the benefit of themselves and the group. When appropriate, gently draw them out: (1) What happened? (2) Who was involved? (3) How did you feel at the time, and after the event? (4) Why do you think things turned out as they did? (5) Were you surprised by anything that transpired? Why? (6) What do you wish would have happened instead? What could you have done differently? (7) What things did you learn from this experience about yourself, your spouse, or your marriage?

Handling Potential Problems

- If nobody talks. In general, don't be afraid of silence, even long stretches of it. Adults need a certain amount of "space" as they think about how to respond to a discussion question. Usually, the silence is a productive, thinking kind. But if you sense that the silence indicates confusion or lack of interest, either rephrase your question or move on to the next one.

- If someone dominates discussion. Occasionally you will have an over-talker in a group. Try some indirect solutions to this problem first. Avoid eye contact after asking a question, or say something like, "Let's hear from others who have been a bit more quiet so far." Or "How do the rest of you respond to Jack's comment?" If indirect methods fail to solve the problem, try a more direct approach. After the study you may need to pull this person aside and say: "I've noticed how enthused you are about participating in the discussion. Great! But I'm concerned about giving everyone a chance to speak."
- If discussion drifts and loses focus. Gently point out that the discussion has moved off track. However, ask the group if this "bunny trail" really is something they want to pursue. Perhaps the issue is important enough to merit significant discussion.
- If people are unfamiliar with the Bible. Some or all of the participants may have very little Bible background. Fine —here is a chance for them to learn! Let the group know from the beginning that no comment or question will be considered "stupid" or inappropriate. Consistently demonstrate that no one needs to be embarrassed by a lack of knowledge or by feeling misinformed. And do acknowledge each contribution. If someone directly espouses a serious doctrinal error, simply say: "Thank you for your contribution, but were you aware that most Christians have understood it this way . . . ?"
- This study group is not psychotherapy and should never be offered as a substitute for professional, medical, or psychological care. If members of the group begin to display high levels of emotional discomfort or marital distress, they should be urged to seek immediate medical, psychological, or pastoral care. Your minister or pastoral care person should be able to assist you in locating competent referral resources.

Evaluating Your Group Experience

You will become a better group leader over the years if you take time to evaluate each of your group leading experiences. This can be done after a series of group sessions (like these six), or at any time during the duration of the study series. Use questions like the following as a personal checklist of your growth in group leadership skills:

____ Did I see any indications of personal and spiritual growth among the members of the group? Describe specific details.

____ Did I enjoy my role as a group facilitator?

____ Was I consistently sensitive to the needs of individuals in the group?

____ Was I able to exercise sufficient flexibility in my plans for each meeting, in order to meet the needs of the group?

____ What were my strengths?

____ What were my weaknesses? How do I know? What can I do to improve next time?

____ To what extent was I prepared and/or unprepared each week?

____ What can I do to improve my preparedness in future group leadership?

____ What feedback did I get from participants during the course of the study series? What specific comments do I remember?

____ Do I feel personally affirmed in my role of group leader? Why?

____ Am I growing in love for people and commitment to the group process as a means of discipling others? How do I know?

The following notes refer to questions in the studies in this book:

Study 1. What Are the Passages of Marriage?
2 Peter 1:2–8

Aim: To introduce the concept of marriage passages and their related tasks.

Question 1. Peter understood that new believers in Christ may begin with an enthusiasm that could wear off if they were not diligent in continuing to develop their spiritual lives. Moral progress was essential. As one wise Christian put it: "The Christian life must not be an initial spasm followed by a chronic inertia."

Help your group members to see the parallels between Christian growth and the growth of their marital relationships. Those relationships, too, must be nurtured and "added to" with knowledge, self-control, patience, and so on. The initial wonder, or infatuation, of Young Love does wear off. But a deeper love can begin to shine through.

Question 3. If God has given us "all things that pertain to life" then we can assume we have the resources and strength from Him to fulfill our marital roles in the most excellent way. However, this does not mean that our spouses will also rely on those same resources. This can cause us pain when we realize that we can only contribute our own best and hope that our spouses will respond in kind. Sometimes that does not happen. Encourage your group members to talk about how they, personally, find strength in God's help and promises without resorting to trying to change their spouses.

Question 4. Change always produces stress, but that stress can be creatively channeled toward adjustments that result in a stronger marriage. Sometimes change brings about a painful reassessment of the marital situation. That pain, though, is "good" in that it brings to light a sore spot that needs to be treated and allowed to heal. Marriages that remain inflexible to change do not experience such opportunities for healing. They may remain "safe" but dull for the time being, until the pressure builds and boils over.

Question 5. Invite volunteers to share specific "clinkers" they have either experienced or anticipate happening in the future. You may wish to have couples discuss together in private some possible solutions to the problem areas they identified.

Question 6. The original Greek term for "add to" (in verse 5) has "chorus" as its root word. The term originally described the actions of wealthy Greek patrons of the performing arts. They would spend large sums of money to provide for the choruses used in the popular stage plays. These people would spare no expense, lavishly equipping the acting troupes. In the same way, Peter calls believers to lavishly equip their souls. This will take some hard work. In the same way, marital partners must come to see that in equipping their marriages with the necessary knowledge and skills to navigate the passages, they should spare no expense or energy.

Question 8. This question could form the basis for an extended "case study" discussion. Ask group members to envision themselves in the same situation as Rick and Jenny. What would they do as a first step toward solving their problems? Be sure to ask for, and discuss, specific ideas.

Study 2. Task One: Mold into One Family.
Genesis 2:18–25

Aim: To identify and analyze the challenges of molding two marriage partners into one family unit.

Question 3. Verse 24 clearly reveals God's desire that the marital relationship be a new creation that leaves father and mother in their proper place. Both couples function as husband and wife in their own households while benefiting from the parent-child relationship in new ways. This is not to suggest that the parental relationship be denied or cut off. But a healthy adjustment recognizes the important new boundaries that have been established for the good of both households.

Question 4. Note that physical and emotional intimacy can hardly be separated in a healthy marriage. No doubt some persons do seek desperately to separate them, going from one sexual partner to the next in a round of purely physical experiences. But this approach to other human beings proves ultimately unsatisfying and eventually resembles sexual addiction more than real intimacy.

Point out that one of the tasks in the Young Love passage is to recognize that the brain is the most important sex organ (see study #4).

Question 5. Adam and Eve surely eventually recognized that they needed to maintain a relationship with their Creator. This is one of the crucial "third legs." Group members may suggest other requirements for marital "completeness," such as maintaining a healthy relationship with parents, submitting to the laws and standards of their community, working with employers to improve job performance, experiencing fellowship in a local church group, maintaining friendships with other couples and neighbors, and so on. Each of these items suggests that a couple still need others, even when they feel as though "just having each other is enough."

Question 7. Point out that our love hunger does not just go away when we finally become adults. Early unmet needs for attention and affection tend to stick with us and constantly fight for expression. So we find ourselves playing out our plea "Please comfort me, Mommy/Daddy!" with our spouses.

Perhaps Jerry and Julia could have found ways to work out this difficulty on their own. Yet, anyone in Julia's situation should feel free to work on love hunger with the help of professional counseling. Ask your adults to give their practical suggestions for how they might have responded as Jerry and Julia. Do not be afraid to suggest that at any time in a marriage, when the going gets rough, it is always appropriate to seek professional guidance from a third party.

Study 3. Task Two: Stop Jockeying for Control.
John 13:3–17

Aim: To identify and analyze the role of Christlike servanthood in resolving marital conflict.

Question 1. This passage is a powerful statement of servanthood because it so clearly affirms the deity of Jesus. He knew that the Father had given all things into His hands; He had come from God; He was going to God (v. 3). Yet at a moment when Jesus might have exercised the most personal power, He showed supreme humility. True love is like that.

Help your group members realize that this kind of love—a willingness to let go of pride at crucial, decisive moments when everything tells us to hold on to it—can go a long way toward making a marriage work beautifully. Such servanthood can come into play when spouses know they have the power and the "right" to assert themselves, but choose not to use that power or to exercise that right. This is a form of love gift.

Question 2. Peter protests what Jesus is about to do, wanting to control the situation. His opposition is couched in the strongest form of negation in the Greek language, literally, "No, no, not, never!" Peter seems to repudiate the Lord as He is and demand that He be a different Lord.

Often marital conflict arises when spouses want each other to change and be different than they are. However, all correction begins and ends in me. I am the only one that I can change.

Question 3. The Christian idea of leadership could be expressed as an inverted pyramid. The one who is the greatest willingly takes the position of the most humble.

In this scene, the disciples had come directly off the street. Normally, a servant would have washed the dust off their feet as they entered the room. However, because this meeting was secret, there was no servant. Yet not one of the disciples willingly took on this humble task. (Actually, they probably had just been arguing about who was to be considered the greatest; see Luke 22:24). No one volunteered to be considered "inferior."

Question 4. A mistake of those in Young Love is to assume that the little irritations of courtship will disappear because "I'll be able to change him/her once we're married." Just the opposite! The little irritations soon escalate into major confrontations. There's no going home (to separate homes) after the date. Now it's time to deal directly with those factors that keep throwing the couple into conflict.

Question 6. Being open and honest can cause conflict when the couple are finally willing to test the strength of the relationship by not covering over real feelings of frustration, resentment, and anger. Yet such honesty is always preferable to a "fake" relationship based on hiding true feelings. When a couple learn how to fight, honesty helps them break through the superficial barriers to deeper intimacy.

Question 7. This quote brings out a crucial concept. Dogs cannot learn to argue their points; they go for the personal attack. Point out that couples can take time to think, realize that they have different points of view, and argue them to resolution. They should not be frightened into isolation by the feeling that they must avoid attacking each other, because conflict need not mean personal attack.

Study 4. Task Three: Build a Sexual Union. 1 Corinthians 7:3–9

Aim: To explore what it means to build a fulfilling sex life that includes life-long intimacy and romance.

Question 1. The Greek word that Paul uses here for our "affection" actually means "duty," "obligation," or "debt." It refers to the obligation to be open to each other for sexual relations. Stress that a couple cannot know how well they are meeting each other's needs in this area unless they communicate candidly with each other about it.

Question 2. Scripture teaches in verses 3-6 that regular sexual relations should prevail because the bodies of the marriage partners belong to each other. My spouse's authority over my body does not mean that I have no right to refuse sex when I do not want it. It does mean that my spouse has "exclusive claim" to my body for sexual intimacy. No one else has that kind of authority over me.

Question 3. Couples end up depriving each other for a number of reasons that usually stem from dysfunctions in their own relationship or in the relationships of their families of origin. Some of the examples mentioned in the book *Passages of Marriage* include possible physical problems, various sexual taboos picked up in the family of origin, childhood sexual abuse that blocks sexual expression as an adult, suppressed or repressed resentment toward a spouse, lack of knowledge about the anatomy of sex, and not dealing with the emotional pain of an abortion.

Question 4. Suggest that this question, along with Question 5, may provide the basis for an extended private conversation between couples interested in improving their sexual communication. Couples could simply share their responses with each other to begin the conversation.

Question 7. The terms reinforce the point that sex must be more than a physical pleasure if it is to become part of a lasting, fulfilling bond between two people in marriage. The physical pleasure is important, of course, but the coming together of genitals can also demonstrate a "meeting of the souls" in which each partner has become open and vulnerable to the other on every level.

**Study 5. Task Four: Make Responsible Choices.
1 Corinthians 7:3–9**

Aim: To consider the benefits of making responsible choices in Young Love.

Question 1. Supply your group members with some biblical background on this passage. In general, during this period of Roman and Greek history, marriage unions were considered fairly impermanent. Corinth was notorious for its lax standards of sexual morality, allowing prostitution and adultery to flourish. To be called a "Corinthian" was equivalent to being called a sexual deviate!

Christians were to be different from the society at large in regard to sexual morality and marriage. In verse 8 of this chapter, Paul stated that for the unmarried to remain so was a "good" thing, if one could stay self-controlled sexually. But for those who were married, to stay married was not just "good," it was a command that had been spoken by the Lord Jesus (see Matt. 5:32; 19:3–9; Luke 16:18).

The point of the double command in verses 10 and 11 is that neither a Christian wife nor a Christian husband should destroy the marriage bond they have entered. This does not deny that almost every married person has had at least fleeting moments of fantasizing a release from the marriage. Discussing these urges with a spouse should never be considered off limits. Better, a couple should consider bringing in a professional third party for counseling when the urge to "abandon ship" gets too strong.

Question 2. In Paul's day, as in ours, marriages often broke up because a dissatisfied spouse wanted to marry another. But this is not allowed in Scripture (see Matt. 19:9). Here, Paul says there are only two options for someone who has already separated for the wrong reasons: (1) Let her or him remain unmarried or (2) be reconciled to her or his spouse.

Question 3. There are a number of reasons why a man divorcing for a "new love" would be making an unwise decision: (1) he's leaving a wife and children to whom he has obligations—and who can bring him happiness, too; (2) he's projecting his own frustrations and shortcomings on his wife; (3) he never made it past Young Love in the first marriage, so probably won't in the second either; (4) he's treating the First Passage as a feel-good-if-you-do-it option rather than as a requirement for marital happiness. Your group members can suggest other reasons, perhaps based on their own experiences.

Question 5. Some "branches" and "deadwood" your group members may suggest are: (1) refusing to move to greater depths of intimacy or vulnerability; (2) succumbing to the fear of entrapment and opting for divorce; (3) resisting change and not adjusting; (4) pretending that problem areas in the marriage don't exist, thereby forfeiting significant communication; (5) failing to find practical ways to keep the romance alive; (6) not adjusting to the surprises of the "real" spouse when the newness of marriage wears off.

Questions 8 and 9. Invite volunteers to talk about early disillusionments they've experienced as the newness of married life wore off. But be careful that the sharing does not turn into a mutual accusation match. Encourage couples to share their own feelings and how they have handled them. Also invite examples of ways couples have successfully dealt with their "real spouse" surprises.

Study 6. Task Five: Deal with Your Parents' Passages. Ephesians 6:1–4

Aim: To discover the unfinished business inherited from parents and determine how to give it back.

Question 1. Obeying and honoring parents is part of the divine law (see the Fifth Commandment, Exod. 20:12). To obey means to listen to parental advice; to honor is to respect and to esteem. The important thing is to discover how to do these things while recognizing that we have been hurt to some extent (usually unintentionally) by our parents.

Your group members may suggest practical ways of continuing to honor their parents even as they themselves move into adulthood. For instance, we could listen respectfully to parents' opinions about the "battle of the sexes" while working to develop our own, perhaps healthier, opinions.

Questions 2 and 3. These questions ask for examples from participants' lives about frustration or anger they've experienced upon discovering the effects of their parents' unfinished business. Remind your group members that this is not to be a blame-casting, parent-bashing session. Since our parents have had to struggle with their parents' unfinished business, too, there really is no blame to assign. The point is to understand the negative influences that have come into our marriages and to do something about them.

Point out that Paul's command to look out for children's welfare (in v. 4) would have been quite revolutionary. In the Roman world the principle of *patria potestas* made the father literal "owner" of his children, with the right to do anything with them that he chose (even to kill them). According to the ancient Roman statesman Seneca: "We slaughter a fierce ox; we strangle a mad dog . . . children who are born weakly and deformed we drown." A letter from a Roman husband to his wife in 1 B.C. stated: "If—good luck to you!—you have a child, if it is a boy, let it live; if it is a girl, throw it out." (Both quotations are from the Daily Study Bible, *Ephesians,* by William Barclay.)

Question 4. Couples should thoroughly discuss this question between themselves in private. Stress that just because we become aware of the reasons for some of our choices, this does not mean they were the wrong choices. A knowledge of motives—conscious and unconscious—can help marriage partners communicate more realistically and adjust to each other with more skill.

Questions 7 and 8. Studies in social psychology and religion have shown that a big influence on adult God-images comes from parents. To young children, Mother and Father are like gods—they can do no wrong; their word is ultimate truth. Early experiences of church life also have a profound effect. One little girl, upon opening the front door to a ministerial couple, shouted: "Mommy, it's God and his wife!"

Work with your group members to ferret out what images of God are warped and distorted by negative family influences. Offer your own spiritual story as a means of suggesting avenues of spiritual growth. But remember that this is ultimately a personal journey that must be taken up in the manner, and in the time, most comfortable for the couples involved.